The Joy of Thinking

Mathematical and Scientific Thinking Skills for Young Minds

Glenn Dee

 FriesenPress

One Printers Way
Altona, MB R0G 0B0
Canada

www.friesenpress.com

ISBN
978-1-03-911030-4 (Hardcover)
978-1-03-911029-8 (Paperback)
978-1-03-911031-1 (eBook)

1. Juvenile Nonfiction, Science & Nature

Distributed to the trade by The Ingram Book Company

ACKNOWLEDGEMENTS

I want to thank God for the knowledge, wisdom, and guidance that I have been blessed with. This book has become a reality because of His blessings. Due to my lack of sight, I must acknowledge and give sincere thanks to those who assisted me in the completion of my book: Shallen Paul-Damon and Marvin Paul for initiating my project and for their commitment to its development in its formative stages; my children Ginette Ferris and Marcel Dee who used their computer knowledge and skills in the creation of various aspects within the book; Madge Paul for her constant inspiration and encouragement for me to realize my dream; and Michael Caille for his patience and dedication in putting my ideas, thoughts, and words on paper, as well as all of the contributions he made to the script, in addition to being my transcriber.

INTRODUCTION

A person who thinks effectively displays these attributes: organization, vision, wisdom, and a passion for learning.

In my book, *The Joy of Thinking*, by using mathematical and scientific principles, I will develop these attributes within the young minds of the readers. These will be used to enhance their natural curiosity, knowledge, and insights. This will assist them in developing their observational, analytical, creative, and critical thinking skills. By using a small and finite data set, the names and the spelling of the names of the ten digits within the decimal system (ZERO, ONE, TWO, THREE, FOUR, FIVE, SIX, SEVEN, EIGHT, NINE), the student can focus on enhancing these thinking skills, without the anxiety often associated with mathematical and scientific studies.

Effective thinking will become as natural and effortless as breathing!

WORKBOOK OBJECTIVES

To complete the activities in this workbook, you will:

1. Learn the importance of developing your observational skills;

2. learn how the data that you have observed can be formatted in various ways to assist you in extracting different information;

3. learn how to interpret and develop the general properties within this information;

4. discover how to form conclusions efficiently by using the various formats and their properties when solving the puzzles;

5.   a. develop the knowledge that will clarify when you have sufficient information to form your conclusion, and

   b. learn to not form conclusions without the necessary and sufficient information to do so;

6. develop a comfort level with your new critical thinking skills, which you will find useful when encountering many new challenges in life;

7. and, very importantly, HAVE FUN.

Thinker B

DigitLand →

Mannie

Thinker O

1

CHAPTER ONE

Mannie: Hi, my name is Mannie, and these are my friends Thinker O and Thinker B. We all want to welcome you to Digitland, which is a fun place with lots of laughter where you will learn to enhance your thinking skills.

Thinker B: This will be done by using the names, the spelling of the names, and the letters used to spell the names of the ten digits (0–9) in our decimal system. We call this our data set.

Thinker O: I will take this data and place it in a format for you to carefully examine. We will call this Chart 1.

CHART 1

ZERO	ONE	TWO	THREE	FOUR	FIVE	SIX	SEVEN	EIGHT	NINE
0	1	2	3	4	5	6	7	8	9
	I	II	III	IIII	II III	III III	III IIII	IIII IIII	IIII IIIII

Mannie: I will be using the data in these charts to create puzzles that will challenge you.

Thinker O: As you have seen with Chart 1, I will create a variety of formats (charts) of the data, which you can, and should, always use as tools when you are solving any of Mannie's puzzles.

Thinker B: When you are examining the data, I will always be there to assist you.

Thinker O: When examining Chart 1, row 2, you will see the ten digit symbols (0–9). Directly above them, in Row 1, are the names of the ten digit symbols. Directly below them, in Row 3, are the values in ones of each of the ten digit symbols. Now that you have examined the data in Chart 1, for your first step, we encourage you to learn the proper spelling of the ten digit names. You will observe that the ten names are spelled using a total of forty letters. You can verify this by counting the number of letters yourself. You will also observe that among the forty letters, there are no A's, no B's ... in fact, there are several letters in the alphabet that are not found in the spelling of the ten digit names! Upon examining the spelling of the ten digit names, you will find that there is a total of fifteen letters of the alphabet that are used.

It is also necessary for you to study the associations between the names, the symbols, and the values in ones for each of the ten digits.

Thinker O: I have made an interesting observation!

Mannie: What is it, Thinker O?

Thinker O: I see a connection between the number of ones and the names associated with each of the ten digits.

Thinker B: What is that connection?

Thinker O: Okay. Let's use the digit 6 as an example. How many ones does this digit have?

Thinker B: It has six ones.

Thinker O: And what is the name given to this symbol?

Thinker B: SIX.

Thinker O: Let's look at a second example, the digit 3. How many ones does this symbol have?

Thinker B: It has three ones.

Thinker O: And what is the name given to this symbol?

Mannie: THREE.

We see the connection! Do you?

Thinker O: The name given to each digit symbol is the same as its value in ones. For example, 5 is called FIVE because it has five ones. The digit 2 is called TWO because it has 2 ones. Is that clear to you? If not, take your time and think about it.

Thinker B: Now let's play a game to see what you have learned so far. The rules of the game are that I am going to take some letters used to spell the ten digit names, and I will form some simple words. You tell me the minimum number of digit names needed, from which you take letters to spell these words. Let's look at an example. How about the word IN? The two letters used to spell the word IN can both be found in the digit name NINE. So the solution is that you will only need one digit name. Let's look at another example. This time the word is ROW. On examining the ten digit names, we find that all three of these letters will not be found in the spelling of any one name. We do see that the letters O and W can be found in the name TWO. The letter R can be taken from one of the three names—ZERO, THREE, or FOUR. So the solution is that you will need a minimum of two names.

Here are some words for you to investigate. Tell me the minimum number of digit names needed to spell them: we, he, or, go, so, it, no, us.

Note: the answers to the investigations presented to you within all of the chapters, with completed charts and necessary information, can be found at the end of Chapter 6.

Now that you have found the answers, how did you do?

Thinker B: Well done! And a big congratulations from all of us!

Now let's kick it up a notch! Here are some more words for you to investigate to find the minimum number of digit names needed to spell them: her, fit, nut, host, our, hen, she, ore, soft, ghost, vixen.

Now that you know these answers, how did you make out this time? We hope you did just as well! If any of your answers don't match, go back and take a second look.

Mannie: Let's conclude this game with three challenging puzzles that I created:

1. We would like you to find two digits under the following conditions:
   a. The sum of the value in ones equals 5.
   b. On examining the letters used to spell the two digit names, you will find exactly 1 E.

Note: you can never use any one digit or digit name more than one time when you are solving any of the puzzles or challenges.

2. We are looking for a digit name spelled with four letters. On examination of the letters used to spell the name, we see that there are no E's.

3. We now would like you to find two digits under the following conditions:

   a. The sum of the two values in ones equals 8.

   b. On examining the letters used to spell the two digit names, you will find exactly 1 O, but you will not find an S.

Thinker B: How did you do with these three puzzles? We hope that you have the same solutions as we do. If you don't, we suggest that you reexamine Chart 1.

Mannie: We sure hope that you had as much fun observing and investigating the data as we had presenting it to you!

Thinker O: We have said that we are going to help you along in developing your thinking skills. I know that the next chart that I have created will assist you when solving all of Mannie's puzzles. We will introduce you to a different format of your data.

Mannie: I know how well Thinker O develops these new formats for the data set. I'm sure that when you use all of your observation skills to study it, my job to create challenging puzzles for you will become much more difficult!

Thinker B: I can't wait to see your new chart, Thinker O!

2
CHAPTER TWO

Thinker O: Although you will be using all of the different formats of the data set when solving Mannie's puzzles, pay special attention to this chart below. You will find that it is extremely important, and that the information you will observe is related to all of the other formats. This chart will be referred to in challenges and your investigations more than any of the other charts.

And now, here it is!

CHART 2

COLUMN 1	COLUMN 2	COLUMN 3
Names with three letters	Names with four letters	Names with five letters
ONE TWO SIX	ZERO FOUR FIVE NINE	THREE SEVEN EIGHT

	COLUMN 1	COLUMN 2	COLUMN 3	
Number of letters used	9	16	15	Total = 40 letters

Thinker O: As you can see, by changing the format of the data between Chart 1 and Chart 2, we still retain the same ten digit names and the forty letters used to spell them.

Thinker B: By carefully observing the information, you can convince yourself of this!

Thinker O: What are some of the similarities and differences that you observe between Chart 1 and Chart 2?

You will notice that the chart is divided into three columns. Column 1 shows three digit names that are each spelled with three letters, Column 2 shows four digit names that are each spelled with four letters, and Column 5 shows three digit names that are each spelled with five letters. It also shows how many letters are used in each column, adding up to forty letters.

In the challenges and puzzles in the book, when you are asked to find two names with a total of six letters, you will find both names in Column 1. When you are asked to find two names with a total of ten letters, you will find both names in Column 3. These are the minimum (six) and the maximum (ten) number of letters needed to spell a combination of two digit names.

Mannie: We now ask you to investigate Chart 2 to determine in what column, or columns, you will find two digit names that are spelled with a total of seven letters, eight letters, and nine letters.

Reminder: answers are found at the end of Chapter 6. You may wish to bookmark the pages.

Thinker B: We know that your answers will be very similar to our answers! Now that you have come to your conclusions for a total of seven letters, eight letters, and nine letters, you see that the solution for eight letters is different from the rest. If you haven't noticed this difference, you should reinvestigate Chart 2.

You have now carefully examined the data in Chart 2. You can now confirm that when adding two digit names for a total of 6, 7, 9, and 10 letters, there is only one solution, whereas with eight total letters, there are 2 solutions.

Mannie: We are now going to present you with some statements. By examining Chart 2, determine whether each statement is TRUE or FALSE.

a. A name spelled with three letters will always be found in Column 1.   T/F

b. The four names in Column 3 are each spelled with five letters.   T/F

c. The letter F will always be found in Column 1 and Column 2.   T/F

d. The total number of letters used to spell two names in Column 1 is 6.   T/F

e. Any two names taken from the same column will be spelled with an equal amount of letters.   T/F

f. Two names that are spelled with a total of nine letters will sometimes be found in Column 2 and Column 3 on Chart 2.   T/F

g. The letter R will only be found in the names in Column 2 and Column 3.   T/F

h. Two names that are spelled with a total of eight letters will always be found in Column 2.   T/F

i. The letter E and the letter N are the only two letters found in names in all columns.   T/F

j. The letter H will only be found in names in Column 3.   T/F

k. When you combine two digit names with a total of eight letters, one of the letters will always be an E.   T/F

Mannie: I have created a few puzzles to test your observation skills.

1. What is the minimum number of digit names required to find the following combinations of letters?

    a. T, R, E   **d.** T, F, S   **g.** H, F, N

    b. F, H   **e.** O, H   **h.** T, H, I

    c. H, S, N   **f.** H, F, S

2. Find the letter, or letters, that are combined with the least amount of the other letters in the spelling of the digit names.

3.   **a.** Find the number of letters that will combine with the letter I when spelling some of the digit names.

      b. Name the letters that you will not find combined with the letter I in the spelling of the digit names.

Thinker B: We are sure that you have answered the above puzzles and the true or false questions correctly. If not, reexamine Chart 2.

Thinker O: We hope that Chart 2 has shown you that by placing the same data in a new format, you can extract new information that you might not have seen before. This chart that we have just investigated only has the spelling of the ten digit names. We want to emphasize that the data observed in all of the various formats is equally important!

Thinker O: Have I got another interesting observation for you! When examining the ten digits in Chart 1, I observed that the digit 4 has the same number of letters in the spelling of its name as its value in ones.

Thinker B: Wow! That's thought-provoking!

Mannie: Well, you know what? I'm going to take this a step further and assign the number zero to that particular observation. And that leads us into Chapter 3!

3

CHAPTER THREE

Thinker O: Why do you think that Mannie chose the number zero for my observation that the digit 4 has the same number of letters in its spelling as its value in ones?

Thinker O: I got it! Mannie has given the digit 4 a value of zero because the number of letters in its name equals its value in ones.

Thinker B: Well, what do you think Mannie will do when a digit has an unequal amount of letters and ones?

Thinker O: We see that Mannie is making a comparison between the number of letters in its name and the number of ones for each digit. If Mannie sees that the digit has more letters in its name than its value in ones, it will be assigned a negative value. Conversely, if the number of ones exceeds the number of letters, Mannie will assign that digit a positive value.

Thinker B: Okay, let's look at some examples together. The digit 1 has three letters in its name, and the number of ones is one. A comparison shows us that the digit 1 has more letters than ones. So, it will be given a negative value. That value will be the difference between these two numbers. In this case, it will be 3−1=2. Therefore, the value assigned to the digit 1 is -2.

Our next example will be the digit 6. Its name is spelled with three letters and the number of ones is six. Because there are more ones than letters, this digit is given a positive value. That value will be the difference between 6 and 3 (6−3=3). Therefore, the value assigned for the digit 6 is +3.

Thinker O: What name should we give to these values?

Thinker B: I know! We can call them Mannie's Numbers!

Thinker O: As you will now see, I have created a new format, including *some* of the new data that we have just examined.

CHART 3

	ZERO	ONE	TWO	THREE	FOUR	FIVE	SIX	SEVEN	EIGHT	NINE
	0	1	2	3	4	5	6	7	8	9
		I	II	III	IIII	II III	III III	III IIII	IIII IIII	IIII IIIII
Mannie's Number		-2			0		+3			

Thinker B: It's thinking time! It will be fun for you to challenge yourself to fill in the Mannie's Number for each of the remaining digits on Chart 3.

Thinker O: Check the answer pages after Chapter 6 to ensure that you have completed the chart correctly. We are sure that you did, but if any of your Mannie's Numbers differ from ours, you should double-check your work.

Thinker B: Isn't it exciting to learn something new? We now want to test and expand on your understanding of Mannie's Numbers. We will start with the digits 5 and 2. The digit 5 has a Mannie's Number of +1 and the digit 2 has a Mannie's Number of -1. Combining the two digits will give you a Mannie's Number of 0. This means that the total number of letters in this combination should equal the total number of ones. Let's check it out! FIVE is spelled with four letters, and TWO is spelled with three letters, for a total of seven letters. FIVE has five ones and TWO has two ones, for a total of seven ones.

Thinker O: Wow! It worked!

Thinker B: Now let's try this with the digits 8 and 4. FOUR is spelled with four letters, and EIGHT is spelled with five letters, for a total of nine letters. Now, by adding the number of ones associated with these two digits, you get a total of twelve in this combination. By comparing the number of ones to the number of letters, we have an excess of three ones. This gives us a Mannie's Number of +3. Let's see what we get when we combine the individual Mannie's Numbers for the digits 8 and 4. The Mannie's Number for 8 is +3, and for 4 is 0. Adding these two gives us +3, which is in agreement with our above calculations. This shows that the value of Mannie's Number will be maintained when combining two or more individual digits.

Mannie: Let me give you three puzzles to solve.

1. We have two digits. The number of ones adds up to 9. The Mannie's Number associated with the combination of these two digits is +1. What is the total number of letters in the two names?

2. We have two digits with a total of seven letters in their names. The Mannie's Number associated with this combination of the two digits is -1. What is the total number of ones in this combination?

3. A combination of two digits gives you a Mannie's Number of +3. A different combination of two digits gives you a Mannie's Number of -6. What can you tell us about each of the combinations, including an example?

Mannie: Let me give you one last brain teaser. Alex and Olivia were having a conversation on this subject. Olivia was telling Alex that she found three individual digits, each with a Mannie's Number of -5, +5, and +4. Alex debated with her that a Mannie's Number of +5 is possible, but not a -5 or a +4. Olivia is sticking to her story! Who is right?

Thinker O: We want to make sure that you are completely comfortable with Mannie's Numbers. Now is the time to go back and examine the information if you have any questions.

Thinker B: Wow! Look how much we have accomplished since first observing the simple and finite data in Chart 1. We are about to make your life much simpler by introducing you to a different format of the data.

4
CHAPTER FOUR

Thinker O: This chapter is slightly different than what we were doing previously. We will be examining the fifteen letters of the alphabet that are found within the forty letters used to spell the ten digit names

FREQUENCY GRAPH

DISTRIBUTION OF THE 40 LETTERS USED
TO SPELL THE DIGIT NAMES

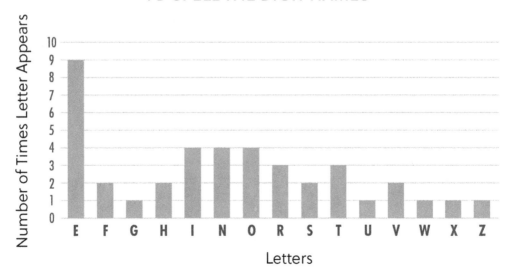

Thinker O: We want to draw your attention to the Frequency Graph. This graph shows you the fifteen letters of the alphabet that are used in the spelling of the ten digits' names. You will find these letters along the horizontal scale. Along the vertical scale you will see how many times each one of these letters occurs.

Thinker B: Looking at the letter E, you can see that the column terminates at 9. This means that the letter E occurs nine times in the spelling of the digit names. I added up the numbers at the top of each column above the letters, and my total came to 40. Is my addition correct? What does this number signify?

Thinker O: A common mistake that is made when reading graphs is that some information is extracted that is not actually showing on the graph. This can be hazardous in most situations. We would like you to pay attention to the following examples. The first example is the letter G. The column above the letter G terminates at 1. What does is that tell you? It only tells you that there is one G among the forty letters. Because there is only one choice, the letter G will occur in only one name. We will now look at the letter R as our second example. The column above the letter R terminates at 3. What does that tell us? It only tells us that there are three R's among the forty letters. Period! Take the two examples and the answers given and make a comparison.

Mannie: Okay, it's time to test your understanding of this graph.

a. The column above the letter S terminates at 2   T/F

b. The columns above the letters T and V terminate at the same number.   T/F

c. For any letter whose column terminates at 1, this means that there is only one name containing that letter. T/F

d. The columns above the letters I, N, and O all terminate at 4. What information does this give you?

e. When Sophie made a copy of this Frequency Graph, she included the letter P. The column above the letter P terminates at 0. What do you think Sophie is saying here?

f. The column above the letter E terminates at 9. Does this 9 mean that there are nine digit names with the letter E in their spelling? Explain.

All of the answers will be found at the end of Chapter 6!

Thinker B: We are sure that you did well with these questions!

Congratulations! You are making great progress. Keep up the good work and keep having fun!

5

CHAPTER FIVE

Thinker O: Now let me present you with Chart 4. Or at least *some* parts of Chart 4! This chart summarizes the information from the previous graph and all of your charts.

CHART 4

COLUMN 1	COLUMN 2	COLUMN 3	COLUMN 4
Letters	Amount found	Number of names in which it is found	Names
E	9	7	Zero, One, Three, Five, Seven, Eight, Nine
F	2	2	Four, Five
G	1	1	Eight
H	2	2	Three, Eight
I	4	4	Five, Six, Eight, Nine
N			
O			
R			
S			
T			

Mannie: It looks like you have some work and fun ahead of you as you complete the chart.

Thinker O: To help you, I will explain the heading above each column. Column 1 is the fifteen letters of the alphabet that are used to spell the ten digit names. Column 2 shows the number of times that a specific letter occurs in the spelling of the ten names. Column 3 shows the number of names that each letter is found within. Column 4 gives you the name, or names, where you will find that specific letter.

Thinker B: As you can see, we have completed the chart for the first five letters. You can also see that the next five letters are shown. Use the information from the graph to fill in Column 2 for these letters. Then, use the information from either Chart 1 or Chart 2 to complete Column 3 and Column 4 for these letters. Finally, find the last five letters from the graph and complete the last three columns of Chart 4 for these remaining letters.

Thinker O: To ensure that you have completed Chart 4 correctly, you can do a simple check of Columns 2 and 3. You should notice that for thirteen of the fifteen letters, the numbers in Columns 2 and 3 are the same. The exceptions are the letter E in Column 2 where the number is 9, then in Column 3 the number is 7, the letter N in Column 2 the number is 4, and in Column 3 the number is 3. How does your chart look?

NOTE: The number in Column 2 must always be equal to, or greater than, the number in Column 3. The exception to this rule is that you cannot have a 1 in Column 2 and a 0 in Column 3. That would be contradictory, as it would imply that you found a letter among the forty letters, but did not find a name spelled with that letter.

The Frequency Graph shows the fifteen letters of the alphabet that make up the ten digit names. Moving to Chart 2, we see that these ten names are divided up into three columns (three names in Column 1 with three letters each, four names in Column 2 with four letters each, and three names in Column 3 with five letters each).

Thinker O: Having made these observations, our natural curiosity leads us to ask the following questions:

- How many of the fifteen letters are used to spell the three names in Column 1?

- How many of the fifteen letters are used to spell the four names in Column 2?

- How many of the fifteen letters are used to spell the three names in Column 3?

You will discover that there are three possible ways that the letters have been placed into the three columns on Chart 2. The three possibilities are:

- Letters found in one of the three columns

- Letters found in two of the three columns

- Letters found in all three of the columns

.....HMMMMM

Thinker B: Here, for your viewing pleasure, is Chart 5!

CHART 5

LETTERS	COLUMN 1 CHART 2 Column 1	COLUMN 2 CHART 2 Column 2	COLUMN 3 CHART 2 Column 3
E	✓	✓	✓
F		✓	
G			✓
H			✓
I	✓	✓	✓
N	✓	✓	✓
O	✓	✓	
R		✓	✓
S	✓		✓
T	✓		✓
U		✓	
V		✓	✓
W	✓		
X	✓		
Z		✓	

Thinker O: If a letter occurs in any name in any of the three columns, we have placed a check mark there. Conversely, if the letter is not found in any names in a column, there is no check mark.

As an example, we will use the letter I. You see a check mark in all three columns for this letter. Another example is the letter F. You see a check mark only in Column 2 for this letter. With the letter V, you see a check mark in Column 2 and Column 3. What do each of these examples mean to you? Let's examine this together.

Thinker B: Referring to Chart 2, you see the letter I used in the spelling of a name, or names, in all three of the columns. You also see that the letter F used in the spelling of a name, or names, in only found in Column 2. Finally, you see that the letter V is found in a name in both Column 2 and Column 3.

Looking at Column 1 on Chart 5, you see seven blank spaces associated with seven of the letters. This means that you will never find any of these seven letters in any name in Column 1 on Chart 2. You can also apply this observation of blank spaces to Columns 2 and 3 on Chart 2.

Mannie: Okay, we will now do an investigation of the information in this chapter. We would first like to draw your attention to Chart 4. TRUE or FALSE:

1. The two names in Column 4 that are spelled with the letter H will both be found in Column 3 on Chart 2.   T/F

2. One of the three names in Column 4 that are spelled with the letter R will be found in Column 1 on Chart 2.   T/F

3. Of the four names in Column 4 that are spelled with the letter O, two will be found in Column 1 on Chart 2, two will be found in Column 2 on Chart 2, and one name will also have the letter S in its spelling.   T/F

4. Of the three names in Column 4 that are spelled with the letter N, one will be spelled with the letter I, one will be spelled with the letter O, and the third name will be spelled with neither an I nor an O.   T/F

Thinker B: Now a little further investigation of Chart 4.

Examine the chart below, which was completed by a fellow student. As you read through each row from left to right, you will find entries that are correct, and entries that are incorrect. Find the correct entries, as well as the incorrect entries. For each row in which you find an incorrect entry, or entries, explain what each column in that row tells you. For every incorrect entry that you find, make the necessary corrections.

CHART 4A

Letter	Amount found	Names found	Names found in
U	0	1	FOUR
V	2	1	FIVE, SEVEN
W	1	1	TWO
X	1	0	SIX
Z	0	0	ZERO

Now that you have done your investigation of this chart, let's go through it together.

Of the five rows, four have incorrect entries and one is correct.

Letter U: The 0 in Column 2 says that there are no U's in any of the names. Yet Columns 3 and 4 say that there is one name with the letter U, and that name is FOUR.

Letter V: Column 3 says that there is one name with the letter V. Yet both Columns 3 and 4 refute that statement.

Letter W: This one is correct!

Letter X: Column 3 says that there are no names with the Letter X. Yet both Columns 2 and 4 say something different.

Letter Z: Column 2 says that there is no Letter Z. Column 3 says there are no names spelled with the Letter Z. And yet in Column 4 we find the name ZERO, which is spelled with the letter Z.

You know where to find Chart 4a with the corrected entries!

Thinker O: We will now do a brief summary of Chart 5 before Mannie gets here! Looking at Chart 5, you will find seven empty spaces in Column 1. How does this observation relate to Column 1 on Chart 2? This simply means that the letters associated with the empty spaces are not found in the spelling of any names in Column 1 on Chart 2. You should also make the same relationship between Chart 5 and Chart 2 for Column 2 and Column 3.

Thinker B: Here's Mannie!

Mannie: Time to put on your thinking cap again. I have a couple of puzzles for you.

1. The total number of letters used to spell two digit names is eight. Among the eight letters, you will find an S and an O. In which two columns on Chart 2 would you find these letters?

Thinker B: Let's see how you did by investigating this together.

- Knowing that there are a total of eight letters tells you that there are two possibilities on Chart 2. These are that both letters occur in Column 2, or that one letter occurs in Column 1 and the other in Column 3.

- Looking at the individual letters, the S and the O, and seeing that the letter S never occurs in any name in Column 2, eliminates Column 2 as a possibility as to where you can find both letters.

- You will also see that the letter O will never be found in any name in Column 3, which means that the letter O must be found in Column 1.

- By a simple process of elimination, this tells us that the letter S must come from Column 3.

Mannie: Here's the next puzzle.

2. In the spelling of two digit names, you will find exactly one O and one F. This combination gives you a Mannie's Number of 0. You must determine in which column, or columns, these two letters are found.

Thinker B: Let's again examine this together to compare our solutions.

- First, you can eliminate taking both the letters F and O from the name FOUR, which by itself has a Mannie's Number of 0. So, you must take the letter F from the name FIVE, which has a Mannie's number of +1.

- Next, you must find a name with the letter O, that when in combination with FIVE gives you a Mannie's Number of 0.

- This name is TWO, which is found in Column 1.

The final solution is that one name will come from Column 1 and the other name will come from Column 2.

Thinker B: Way to go! At this pace, you could soon be considered to be one of the Great Thinkers!

Thinker O: I noticed on the Frequency Graph that there are five letters that terminate at 1. On Chart 4, I noticed that those letters are each in five individual names. For these five letters, we came up with the name "unique letters".

Thinker B: Great name! Now let's examine why we call them "unique."

CHAPTER SIX

Thinker O: We are now down to our final investigation. Looking back at Chart 4, we see that in both Columns 2 and 3, there are five letters with the number 1. Reading across to Column 4, you will find these five letters alphabetically in the names EIGHT, FOUR, TWO, SIX, and ZERO. Again, we will call these unique letters. We will now create Chart 6, with Column 1 having the names with unique letters in numerical order (ZERO, TWO, FOUR, SIX, EIGHT). Column 2 will be formed by the remaining 5 names in numerical order (ONE, THREE, FIVE, SEVEN, NINE).

CHART 6

COLUMN 1	COLUMN 2
Names With Unique Letters	**Names Without Unique Letters**
ZERO	ONE
TWO	THREE
FOUR	FIVE
SIX	SEVEN
EIGHT	NINE

Thinker O: We're here together to get you started on your final investigation. Looking at Column 1 on Chart 6, we see three names spelled without the letter E. The remaining two names in this column are spelled with exactly one E. We now shift our attention to Column 2. We see that all five names in this column are spelled with at least one E. Two of the names are actually spelled with two E's. This means that if you see a name spelled *without* the letter E, it will have a unique letter. But if you see a name spelled *with* the letter E, it may, or may not, have a unique letter. Also, any name spelled with two E's will not have a unique letter.

Looking at the chart, we see that some letters are used to spell names in both columns. Some examples are the letters T, F, and S. Our curiosity leads us to investigate whether there are any letters, besides the unique letters, that are found in only one of the two columns. On close examination of the remaining six letters, we find the letters N and V only in the names in Column 2. This means that any name spelled with an N, V, or two E's will not have a unique letter. You can check and verify all of these observations for yourself.

Thinker B: All of these observations will be very important in assisting you when solving the puzzles. There are many other observations that can be found in Chart 6. We encourage you to continue your examination of this chart. The more knowledge that you acquire from these charts, the more comfortable you will become.

Mannie: Here is a challenge for you! Use the letters from two digit names to spell the word FIRE. Examining the letters used to spell the two names, you will find exactly one unique letter, exactly one F, and exactly one E.

Thinker B: Let's go through this together.

- I am looking for two names, and only one is spelled with an E.

- A property of names that are not spelled with an E is that they will have a unique letter. This takes us to Column 1 on Chart 6. The three names are TWO, FOUR, and SIX.

- We know that the second name is spelled with one E, and does not contain a unique letter. This takes us to Column 2. The three names are ONE, FIVE, and NINE.

- We find the letter R, from the word FIRE, only in the name FOUR, which is also spelled with the letter F, and has a unique letter. So, one of the names is FOUR.

- Moving back to the three names in Column 2, we can eliminate the name FIVE, as we have already found the one F needed to spell the word FIRE. The remaining two letters (I and E) can only be found in the name NINE.

So, our final solution are the names FOUR and NINE. With any of the puzzles presented to you, always go back and examine the steps required to get your solution if you are not sure.

Mannie: Now we are going to kick it up a notch again!

You will use some of the letters from two digit names to spell the word FEVER. Examining the letters used to spell the two names, you will find exactly one unique letter. The combination of the two names has a Mannie's Number of -3.

Thinker B: Okay, let's compare our solutions.

- You will find the letter V in Column 2 of Chart 6 in the names FIVE and SEVEN.

- If we take the letters E, V, and E from the name SEVEN, we would then take the letters F and R from the name FOUR. This combination would give us the unique letter, but would not give us the correct Mannie's Number.

- So we must take the letters F, V, and E from the name FIVE, which has a Mannie's Number of +1.

- We must now find a name with the letters E and R, one unique letter, and a Mannie's Number of -4.

Thinker O: I know! I know! The name ZERO covers all the bases!

Mannie: You are correct, Thinker O! So, our final solution are the names ZERO and FIVE.

Thinker B: Isn't thinking joyful? WOW!

ANSWERS FOR CHAPTER 1 THROUGH CHAPTER 6

CHAPTER 1

WE - two names HE - one name
OR - one name GO - two names
SO - two names

IT - one name NO - one name
US - two names

HER - one name FIT - two names
NUT - three names HOST - three
names OUR - one name

HEN - two names SHE - two
names ORE - one name
SOFT - three names

GHOST - three names
VIXEN - two names

1. 1 and 4. Examining both 0 + 5 and 2 + 3, you find two E's in the digit names.

2. FOUR

3. 0 and 8. 1 + 7 one O/one S, 2 + 6 one O/one S, 3 + 5 no O/no S

CHAPTER 2

two names - seven letters Column 1 and Column 2
two names - eight letters Column 1 and Column 3 OR
both names from Column 2
two names - nine letters Column 2 and Column 3

a. TRUE

b. FALSE - only three names in Column 3

c. FALSE - only in Column 2

d. TRUE

e. TRUE

f. FALSE - names always found in Column 2 and Column 3

g. TRUE

h. FALSE - also found in Column 1 and Column 3

i. FALSE - the letter I is also found in all three columns

j. TRUE

k. TRUE

1. **a.** T, R, E - one name   **b.** F, H - two names
   c. H, S, N - two names   **d.** T, F, S - three names
   e. O, H - two names   **f.** H, F, S - three names
   g. H, F, N - three names   **h.** T, H, I - one name

2. You will find both the letter X and the letter W in Column 1, combined with only two other letters.

3. **a.** You will find nine letters.
   b. The remaining five letters are Z, W, U, O, R.

CHAPTER 3

CHART 3

ZERO	ONE	TWO	THREE	FOUR	FIVE	SIX	SEVEN	EIGHT	NINE
0	1	2	3	4	5	6	7	8	9
	I	II	III	IIII	II III	III III	III IIII	IIII IIII	IIII IIIII

	ZERO	ONE	TWO	THREE	FOUR	FIVE	SIX	SEVEN	EIGHT	NINE
Mannie's Number	-4	-2	-1	-2	0	+1	+3	+2	+3	+5

1. Eight letters. The difference between the number of ones (9) and the number of letters (8) gives you the Mannie's Number of +1.

2. Six ones. The difference between the number of ones (6) and the number of letters (7) gives you the Mannie's Number of -1.

3. A Mannie' Number of +3 means that there are three more ones than letters. An example would be the digits five and seven. There are twelve ones in the sum of the two digits, and a total of nine letters in the combination of the names FIVE and SEVEN.

A Mannie's Number of -6 means that there are six more letters than ones. An example would be the digits three and zero. There are three ones in the sum of the two digits, and a total of nine letters in the combination of the names THREE and ZERO.

CHAPTER 4

a. TRUE

b. FALSE - On the Frequency Graph, the letter T terminates at 3, while the letter V terminates at 2.

c. TRUE

d. It ONLY tells you that the letters I, N, and O each occur four times within the spelling of the ten digit names.

e. According to the graph, Sophie is saying that the letter P is not among the forty letters used to spell the ten digit names.

f. No. It only means that there are nine E's among the forty letters.

CHAPTER 5

CHART 4

COLUMN 1	COLUMN 2	COLUMN 3	COLUMN 4
Letters	Amount found	Number of names in which it is found	Names
E	9	7	Zero, One, Three, Five, Seven, Eight, Nine
F	2	2	Four, Five
G	1	1	Eight
H	2	2	Three, Eight
I	4	4	Five, Six, Eight, Nine
N	4	3	One, Seven, Nine
O	4	4	Zero, One, Two, Four
R	3	3	Zero, Three, Four
S	2	2	Six, Seven
T	3	3	Two, Three, Eight
U	1	1	Four
V	2	2	Five, Seven
W	1	1	Two
X	1	1	Six
Z	1	1	Zero

1.　**a.** TRUE

b. FALSE - There are no digit names spelled with the letter R in Column 1 on Chart 2.

c. FALSE - There are no digit names spelled with both the letter S and the letter O.

d. TRUE

CHART 4A CORRECTED

Letter	Amount found	Names found	Names
U	1	1	FOUR
V	2	2	FIVE, SEVEN
W	1	1	TWO
X	1	1	SIX
Z	1	1	ZERO

YOU SURE ARE DOING GREAT ANSWERING MY PUZZLES AND CHALLENGES! THERE'S MORE TO COME. KEEP UP THE GOOD WORK!

HELPFUL HINTS

Thinker B: Before you get started solving Mannie's puzzles, here are some helpful hints and reminders.

1. Always read the question carefully. You must always have a clear understanding of what you are being asked, and what information you are being given.

2. Don't forget to use all of the tools, including the charts, the graph, and all of the properties associated with them, that we have made available to you.

3. Always organize your thoughts regarding the information presented to you. Your first step is to always identify a starting point to work toward when solving any of Mannie's puzzles.

4. Any information that is needed in order to come to a final conclusion is considered to be necessary information. Once you have

enough necessary information to form a final conclusion, you will have sufficient information.

Mannie: Here are a couple of illustrations to emphasize these points.

A star (*) designates a point of necessary information.

Thinker B: We have two digit names that are spelled with a total of eight letters, and three of the letters are H, I, and S.

a. With 100 per cent certainty, could you tell me what name the letter S comes from?

b. With 100 per cent certainty, could you tell me what name the letter H comes from?

- The total of eight letters takes us to Chart 2, with both names coming from Column 2, or one name coming from Column 1 and one name from Column 3. *

- Examining the ten names, there is not one name spelled with both the letters H and S. So, the H must come from one name and the S from another name. *

- A property of Column 2 is that you will never find a name spelled with either the letter H or the letter S. This now eliminates Column 2. *

- A property of Column 3 is that the two names spelled with the letter H (THREE and EIGHT) are found in this column. So, the name spelled with the letter H must come from Column 3. *

- Therefore, the name spelled with the letter S must come from Column 1. *

We now have sufficient information to form a final conclusion.

    a. The answer is yes! The letter S must come from the name SIX. (The letter I can also come from the name SIX).

    b. The answer is no! You would need at least one other piece of information to allow you to choose between the two names THREE and EIGHT.

Thinker O: Got it? We knew that you would! Here's another illustration for you.

Mannie: We have two digit names. We use four letters from these two names to spell the word ROOT. The combination of these two names gives us a Mannie's Number of -1. What are the two names?

- Chart 4 shows me that there are 4 O's, and that each letter O is in a separate name. Therefore, the two digit names will each be spelled with an O. *

- The letters T and R will each be found in separate names. *

- Chart 3 shows me that the letters T and O must come from the name TWO, which has a Mannie's Number of -1. *

- Chart 3 also shows me that the letters R and O come from either the name ZERO, with a Mannie's Number of -4, or the name FOUR, with a Mannie's Number of 0. *

We now have sufficient information to form our final conclusion. One of the names is TWO, which has a Mannie's number -1. The other name must maintain this Mannie's Number of -1. This digit must have a Mannie's number of 0. Therefore, this digit is FOUR, and our final solution is TWO and FOUR.

Thinker B: Okay, one last time. Just remember to always read the question carefully!

Thinker O: Congratulations! You have completed the first part of the book. You will now apply the many skills that you have developed (observation, investigation, creativity, analysis, proper conclusions, etc.) to solve Mannie's challenges and puzzles. Feel free to create your own charts to further break down and investigate the ten digit names. We all hope that you have had as much fun with these activities as we had presenting and investigating them with you!

Note: You will find the answers to the puzzles in Challenges 1–4 at the end of Challenge 4. Some answers will also provide a good first step or other information to assist you with making your conclusions.

CHALLENGE 1

USING THE PRESENCE AND ABSENCE OF INFORMATION TO FIND SOLUTIONS

Mannie: Let's play a game!

Thinker O: Sure! What is the game called, and what are the rules?

Mannie: It's called "My eyes see, my eyes don't see." Here is the explanation:

- You must focus your attention on me. With both of my eyes open, I will reveal a letter, or letters, or other information, that must be used to determine the digit name you are looking for.

- With both of my eyes closed, you will be shown a letter, or letters, or other information, which cannot be used to determine the digit name you are looking for.

Thinker O and Thinker B: Okay, let's play the game!

Thinker B: Using all of your charts and remembering your helpful hints will be of great assistance when you are solving all of these puzzles.

Mannie: Have fun with these challenges, and see yourself gaining confidence as you move forward!

Question number	I SEE	I DON'T SEE	DIGIT NAME
1	H	R	
2	E, E	R	
3	F	Unique Letter	
4	R	O	
5	T	H	
6	+3 Mannie's Number	G	
7	O	Unique Letter	
8	O and E	N	
9	4 letters in a name	E	
10	N and E	O or V	
11	T, H, and E	Unique Letter	
12	+ Mannie's Number	E	
13	Unique Letter	+ or - Mannie's Number	
14	- Mannie's Number	E	
15	T	- Mannie's Number	

Thinker B: Congratulations! That was fun! Are you ready for your next challenge?

CHALLENGE 2

Mannie: Have you ever noticed that you can find the letters used to spell some common words within the spellings of the ten digit names? For example, the letters used to spell the word "or" can be found within the digit names ZERO and FOUR. Here's an example for you to try: The word "hit" is spelled with three letters. All three of the letters can be found in the spelling of one of the digit names. Can you tell me what digit name it is?

Thinker O and Thinker B: We are sure that you came up with the digit name EIGHT! Now you are ready for Challenge 2!

	Given Words	DIGIT NAME
1	ORE	
2	IN	
3	IS	
4	HERE	
5	SEE	
6	TIE	
7	TOW	
8	OUR	
9	ON	
10	IF	
11	INN	
12	THERE	
13	EVEN	
14	FUR	
15	GET	

Thinker B: Well done! Let's keep moving along.

CHALLENGE 3

Mannie: In this challenge, you will be solving these puzzles to determine a specific digit name. In each puzzle, you will be guided to a chart or charts which will help you to determine this name. By carefully observing the information on the charts, and remembering the properties associated with each one, will keep you moving right along.

1. * You are looking for letters to spell this digit name.
   * On Chart 5, there are letters found in only one of the three columns.
   * On Chart 5, there are letters found in two of the three columns.
   * You will be looking for the letters found in all 3 of the columns.

2. * You will not find any unique letters in the spelling of this digit name.
   * One letter you must use will only be found in Column 2 on Chart 2.

3. * The digit name you are looking for is found in Column 2 on Chart 6.
   * The digit name has a Mannie's Number that is both + and even.

4. * You will find a unique letter in the spelling of this digit name.
   * Besides the unique letter, you must also use a letter found only in Column 3 on Chart 2.

5. * The digit name you are looking for has a Mannie's Number that is both - and odd.

6. * One letter you must use to spell this digit name is found only in Columns 1 and 2 on Chart 5.
   * There is no unique letter in the spelling of this name.

7. * The digit name you are looking for is found in Column 1 on Chart 6.
   * One letter you must use to spell this digit's name is an E.
   * This digit name has a - Mannie's Number.

8. * The digit name you are looking for is found in Column 2 on Chart 6.
   * Two of the letters used in the spelling of this name will never be found in any of the names in Column 1 on Chart 6.

9. * The digit name you are looking for is spelled with at least one E.
   * Another letter in its spelling is only found in Columns 2 and 3 on Chart 5.
   * Another letter in its spelling is only found in Column 3 on Chart 5.

10. * In the spelling of this digit name you will not find an E.
    * One letter used in the spelling of this name will be found in all three columns on Chart 5.

11. To spell this digit name:
    * Find all of the letters that are only in both Columns 1 and 3 on Chart 5.
    * You will use only one of these letters.
    * You cannot use any of the letters found in all three columns on Chart 5.

12. To spell this digit name:

    * Find all of the letters that are only in both Columns 2 and 3 on Chart 5.

    * You will use only one of these letters.

    * Find the three letters that are only in Column 2 on Chart 5. Also, find the two letters that are only in Column 3 on Chart 5.

    * You cannot use any of these five letters.

Thinker B: Well done! We illustrated the importance of using the information from the charts, and you met the challenge!

CHALLENGE 4

Mannie: Okay! We know that you are now ready for some real challenges!

1. I am giving you two digit names, THREE and FIVE. Using four of the nine letters, I was able to spell the word EVER. You must use the remaining five letters to spell a word that begins with the letter T. What word is it?

2. I am giving you two digit names, SEVEN and EIGHT. Using five of the ten letters, I was able to spell the word GIVEN. You must use the remaining five letters to spell a word that begins with the letter T. What word is it?

3. I am giving you three digit names, THREE, FOUR, and SEVEN. Using five of the fourteen letters, I was able to spell the word FEVER. You must use the remaining nine letters to spell two words. One word begins with an H, and the other begins with an R. What are the two words?

4. I have used all of the letters from three digit names to spell the words EVER, EXIT, and FISH. What are the three digit names?

5. Shifting your focus back to Chart 3, you will notice that some of Mannie's Numbers are +, some are -, and the digit four is 0. We now have a few challenges for you:

   a. We are looking at two digits whose names are found in Column 1 and Column 3 on Chart 2. The sum of these two digits has a Mannie's Number of -3. What is the sum in ones of these two digits?

b. We are looking at two digits whose names are found in Column 1 and Column 2 on Chart 2. The sum of these two digits is 7. What is Mannie's Number for this combination?

c. The sum of two digits in ones is 11. Would the Mannie's Number for this sum be +, -, 0, or any combination of these?

d. The sum of two digits in ones is 6. Would the Mannie's Number for this sum be +, 0, -, or any combination of these?

6. You will be looking for two digit names. I have used some of the letters from these two names to spell these words. What two digit names did I use?

a.	SIZE	**e.**	FRUIT	**i.**	NOISE
b.	RUIN	**f.**	WORTH	**j.**	FOOT
c.	TWIN	**g.**	SNEEZE	**k.**	SHINE
d.	NORTH	**h.**	NURSE	**l.**	SHIRT

NOTE: When we use the word "set," it refers to a group of two or more digit names. An example of this is: With the word US, how many different sets of digit names can you find to spell this word? You will find two sets: (FOUR, SIX) and (FOUR, SEVEN).

7. How many different sets of two digit names can you find to spell the words:

   a. WE

   b. NOR

   c. HOT

   d. SHIN

   e. FOE

8. I have used some of the letters from two digit names to spell these words. What are the two digit names?

   a. RISE * On examination of the letters used to spell these two names, you will find one unique letter.

   b. ROSE * On examination of the letters used to spell these two names, you will find a total of seven letters.

   c. FUN * The combination of these two digit names will give you a Mannie's Number of +2.

   d. ROW * On examination of the letters used to spell these two digit names, you will find one O.

   e. OVEN * On examination of the letters used to spell these two digit names, you will find one unique letter.
   * The combination of these two digit names will give you a Mannie's Number of -2.

   f. FIT * On examination of the letters used to spell these two names, you will find one unique letter.
   * The letters F, I, and T only appear once.

g. HEIR * On examination of the letters used to spell these two names, you will find one unique letter.
* The total number of letters used to spell these two names is 8.

h. TOO * On examination of the letters used to spell these two names, you will find only one E.
* The combination of these two digit names will give you a Mannie's Number of -3.

i. IS * On examination of the letters used to spell the two digit names, you will find one S and one I.
* The total number of letters used to spell these two names is 8.

9. You will be looking for six digit names! Take one letter from each of the six names to spell the word TOFFEE. Only one of the six names has a unique letter. What are the six names?

10. You will now be looking for three digit names. I have used some of the letters from these names to spell these words. What are the three digit names?

a. SUNG

b. VISION

c. INTEREST

d. WRITTEN

e. HORROR

f. SWING

g. FINISH

h. HORIZON

i. VERSUS

j. FOGHORN

11. With the words below, how many different sets of three digit names can you find to spell each word?

    a. TOXIN   **c.** SOON

    b. NOON   **d.** SHOE

12. Referring back to the previous question, we now want you to list the sets of three digit names that you found for each of the four words.

13. Use some of the letters from three digit names to spell the word SHOE.
The Mannie's Number for this combination of three names is -4. What are the three names?

14. With these words, you will be looking for three digit names, and take two letters from each name:

    a. SHIVER * None of the three names are spelled with the same amount of letters.

    b. FOREST * The three names combined have a Mannie's Number of 0.

    c. FUSION * On examination of the letters used to spell the three names, there is one unique letter.

    d. ZENITH * The three names combined have a Mannie's Number of -1.

e. REFUSE * The total number of letters used to spell the three names is 13.
On examination of these thirteen letters, there is one unique letter.

f. FINGER * The total number of letters used to spell the three names is twelve.

g. FREEZE * Of the letters used to spell the three names, there is one R.

15. **a.** The sum of two digits in ones is 7. Would Mannie's Number for this sum be -,0, +, or any combination of these?

b. The sum of two digits in ones is 8. Would Mannie's Number for this sum be -, 0, +, or any combination of these?

16. How many different sets of three digit names can you find to spell the word FROST:

a. With each set having three unique letters?

b. With each set having two unique letters?

c. With each set having one unique letter?

17. You will be using some of the letters from four digit names to spell the word EXTINGUISH. On examination of the letters used, you will find two E's. The Mannie's Number for this set of four names is +11.

18. You will be looking for five digit names. Take one letter from each of these five names to spell the word RIGHT. On examination of the letters used to spell these names, you will find four E's and four unique letters.

19. You will be looking for three digit names, with a total of twelve letters, to spell the word FISH.
Among the letters, you will find one I.

20. **a.** You will be looking for three digit names to spell the word GNU. Your classmate Bob states that the Mannie's Number for this set of three digit names has a - value.
Is that possible? Explain your answer.

b. You will be looking for two digit names to spell the word ZOO. Your classmate Ginette states that the Mannie's Number for this set of two digit names has a - value. Is that possible? Explain your answer.

21. With these words, you will be looking for three digit names:

a. RUSH * The total number of letters used to spell the three names is 12.
* On examination of the letters used to spell the three names, there are 2 unique letters.

b. ZENITH * The three names combined have a Mannie's Number of +4.

c. GET * On examination of the letters used to spell the three names, there is the unique letter G, there is one E, and there is one T.

d. REFUGE * On examination of the letters used to spell the three names, you will see that the number of E's and the number of unique letters is equal.
* You will be taking two letters from each name.

e. TERROR * You will be taking two letters from each name.

f. WINTER * On examination of the letters used to spell the three names, there is one unique letter.

g. SORT * On examination of the letters used to spell the three names, you will find one unique letter.
* there is one S, one O, one R, and one T.

22. You will be taking one letter from each of four digit names to spell the word TOUR.

a. On examination of the letters used to spell the four digit names, you will find three unique letters. The the Mannie's Number for this set of four digit names is 0.

b. On examination of the letters used to spell the four digit names, you will find two unique letters. The Mannie's Number for this set of four digit names is -8.

23. You will be looking for three digit names:

a. These three names are spelled with a total of eleven letters. Among the eleven letters is one unique letter.
This set of three names has a Mannie's Number of +5.

b. The total in ones for these three digits is 5.
This set of three names has a Mannie's Number of -6.

c. These three names are spelled with a total of thirteen letters.
This set of three names has a Mannie's Number of -6.

d. The total in ones for these three digits is 20.
This set of three names has a Mannie's Number of +7.

24. You will be looking for four digit names. Take one letter from each of these four names to spell the word SURF. There are two unique letters among the letters used to spell the four names. The Mannie's Number for this set of four digit names is -1.

25. You will be looking for four digit names. Take one letter from each of these four names to spell the word TURF. The total number of letters used to spell the four names is 16.

26. You will be looking for three digit names to spell the word WISH. The total number of letters used to spell the three names is 13.

27. When combining two digits, what are the minimum and maximum number of letters you can have in the set of the two digit names?

28. Avril was asked to find the Mannie's Number for two digits that total eleven ones. The answer that she gave was a Mannie's Number with a - value. Comment on Avril's answer.

29. Find the two digit names that you will use to spell each of the following words:

    a. OXEN
           d. GONE

    b. NOISE
          e. STONE

    c. THRONE

30. The sum of two digits in ones is 13. When a third digit is added to the first two digits, the sum remains at 13. The Mannie's Number for this combination is 0. Find the three digit names.

31. The Mannie's Number when you add two digits is 0. When you add a third digit, the Mannie's number remains at 0. The total of all three digits in ones is 11. Find the three digit names.

32. Use two digit names, taking two letters from one name and three letters from the other name to spell each of these words:

    a. SIGHT
          c. TIGHT

    b. NIGHT
          d. RIGHT

33. You will be looking for four digit names that are spelled with a total of seventeen letters. Among the letters, you will find one unique letter, one F, one S, and two T's.

34. Each of these two words, SUIT and SUITE, are spelled using three digit names. Will the letter T come from the digit name TWO in each of the solutions? Explain your answer.

35. With each of the following groups of letters that you will find in three digit names, find the maximum amount of these three names that are *not* spelled with a unique letter.

    a. O, O, I

    b. O, O, I, E Would your answer differ from your previous solution, and if so, how?

    c. O, O, I, E, E (Be careful how you arrange your E's!)

    d. O, O, I, E, E, E

36. Alex and Olivia were looking for three digit names, and among the letters used to spell the names were one O, one E, and two I's. The question was asked as to whether the letter O and the letter E could be combined in one name. Alex said that of course they can, while Olivia stated that this is not possible. Who is right? Explain.

37. Izzy and Jamie were discussing a follow-up to a previous question. Jamie said that you could take one letter from each of five digit names to spell the word TIGHT. Izzy said that was not possible. What is your choice, YES or NO? Explain your choice.

BONUS QUESTIONS

1. A, B, and C are three individual digit names.

A + B = C   A has a unique letter and B does not have a unique letter.

Does C have a unique letter?

2. W, X, Y, and Z are four individual digit names.

X + Y = Z and Y > X   Z has no letter E in its spelling.

Y + Z = W   W does not have a unique letter.

Find the digit names for W, X, Y, and Z.

CHALLENGE ANSWERS

CHALLENGE 1

1. EIGHT

2. SEVEN

3. FIVE

4. THREE

5. TWO

6. SIX

7. ONE

8. ZERO

9. FOUR

10. NINE

11. THREE

12. SIX

13. FOUR

14. TWO

15. EIGHT

CHALLENGE TWO

1. ZERO
2. NINE
3. SIX
4. THREE
5. SEVEN
6. EIGHT
7. TWO
8. FOUR
9. ONE
10. FIVE
11. NINE
12. THREE
13. SEVEN
14. FOUR
15. EIGHT

CHALLENGE 3

1. NINE
2. FIVE
3. SEVEN
4. EIGHT
5. TWO
6. ONE
7. ZERO
8. SEVEN
9. THREE
10. SIX
11. TWO
12. SEVEN

CHALLENGE 4

1. THIEF
2. THESE
3. HOUSE, RENT
4. THREE, FIVE, SIX

5.   **a.** Column 1 and Column 3 totals eight letters. Having eight letters and a Mannie's Number of -3 gives you a sum of five ones.

       b. Column 1 and Column 2 totals seven letters. Having seven letters and seven ones gives you a Mannie's Number of 0.

       c. The maximum number of letters in two digit names is ten. Having ten letters and eleven ones gives you a + Mannie's Number.

       d. The sums of 6 + 0, 5 + 1, and 4 + 2 all equal six ones, with all having a total of seven letters. All of these combinations will give you a - Mannie's Number.

6.   **a.** SIZE   SI - SIX   ZE - ZERO

       b. RUIN   RU - FOUR   IN - NINE

       c. TWIN   TW - TWO   IN - NINE

       d. NORTH   NO - ONE   RTH - THREE

       e. FRUIT   FRU - FOUR   IT - EIGHT

       f. WORTH   WO -TWO   RTH - THREE

       g. SNEEZE   ZE - ZERO   SNEE - SEVEN

       h. NURSE   UR - FOUR   NSE - SEVEN

i. NOISE   NOE - ONE   IS - SIX

j. FOOT   FO - FOUR   OT - TWO

k. SHINE   SNE - SEVEN   HI - EIGHT

l. SHIRT   SI - SIX   HRT - THREE

7.

a. WE   (TWO, ZERO) (TWO, ONE) (TWO, THREE)
(TWO, FIVE) (TWO, SEVEN) (TWO, EIGHT) (TWO, NINE)   7

b. NOR   (ONE, ZERO) (ONE, FOUR) (ONE, THREE)
(SEVEN, ZERO) (SEVEN, FOUR) (FOUR, NINE) (ZERO, NINE) 7

c. HOT   (THREE, ZERO) (THREE, ONE) (THREE, TWO)
(THREE, FOUR) (EIGHT, ZERO) (EIGHT, ONE) (EIGHT, TWO)
(EIGHT, FOUR)   8

d. SHIN   (SEVEN, EIGHT)   1

e. FOE   (FOUR, ZERO) (FOUR, ONE) (FOUR, THREE)
(FOUR, FIVE) (FOUR, SEVEN) (FOUR, EIGHT) (FOUR, NINE)
(FIVE, ZERO) (FIVE, ONE) (FIVE, TWO)   10

8.

a. RISE   THREE, SIX

b. ROSE   ZERO, SIX

c. FUN   FOUR, SEVEN

d. ROW   TWO, THREE

e. OVEN   ZERO, SEVEN

f. FIT   TWO, FIVE

g. HEIR   THREE, SIX

h. TOO   ONE, TWO

i. IS   THREE, SIX

9. TOFFEE   ONE, THREE, FOUR, FIVE, SEVEN, NINE

10.   a. SUNG   FOUR, SEVEN, EIGHT

b. VISION   ONE, FIVE, SIX

c. INTEREST   THREE, SEVEN, EIGHT

d. WRITTEN   TWO, THREE, NINE

e. HORROR   ZERO, THREE, FOUR

f. SWING   TWO, SEVEN, EIGHT

g. FINISH   FIVE, SEVEN, EIGHT

h. HORIZON   ZERO, ONE, EIGHT

i. VERSUS   FOUR, SIX, SEVEN

j. FOGHORN   ONE, FOUR, EIGHT

11. **a.** TOXIN   5 sets

     b. NOON   9 sets

     c. SOON   9 sets

     d. SHOE   16 sets

12. **a.** TOXIN   (TWO, SIX, NINE) (TWO, SIX, ONE) (TWO, SIX, SEVEN) (EIGHT, SIX, ONE) (THREE, SIX, ONE)

     b. NOON   (ONE, ZERO, SEVEN) (ONE, ZERO, NINE) (ONE, TWO, SEVEN) (ONE, TWO, NINE) (ONE, FOUR, SEVEN) (ONE, FOUR, NINE) (ZERO, TWO, NINE) (ZERO, FOUR, NINE) (TWO, FOUR, NINE)

     c. SOON   (SEVEN, ZERO, ONE) (SEVEN, TWO, ONE) (SEVEN, FOUR, ONE) (SIX, ZERO, ONE) (SIX, TWO, ONE) (SIX, FOUR, ONE) (SEVEN, ZERO,TWO) (SEVEN, ZERO,FOUR) (SEVEN, TWO, FOUR)

     d. SHOE   FIRST STEP: I would start by finding the sets, taking the letter S from SIX, and then taking the letter S from SEVEN.
(SIX, THREE, ZERO) (SIX, THREE, ONE) (SIX, THREE, TWO) (SIX, THREE, FOUR) (SIX, EIGHT, ZERO) (SIX, EIGHT, ONE) (SIX, EIGHT, TWO) (SIX, EIGHT, FOUR) (SEVEN, THREE, ZERO) (SEVEN, THREE, ONE) (SEVEN, THREE, TWO) (SEVEN, THREE, FOUR) (SEVEN, EIGHT, ZERO) (SEVEN, EIGHT, ONE) (SEVEN, EIGHT, TWO) (SEVEN, EIGHT, FOUR)

13. The set of ZERO (-4) THREE (-2) and SEVEN (+2) gives you a combined Mannie's Number of -4.

14. **a.** SHIVER   (HR - THREE, VE - FIVE, SI - SIX)

  b. FOREST   (TR - THREE, FO - FOUR, SE - SEVEN)

  c. FUSION   (OU - FOUR, FI - FIVE, SN - SEVEN)

  d. ZENITH   (ZE - ZERO, TH - THREE, NI - NINE)

  e. REFUSE   (UR - FOUR, FE - FIVE, SE - SEVEN)

  f. FINGER   (NE - ONE, FR - FOUR, GI - EIGHT)

  g. FREEZE   (ZR - ZERO, FE - FIVE, EE -SEVEN)

15. **a.** The sum of 0 + 7 gives a Mannie's Number of - 2

1 + 6	+1
2 + 5	0
3 + 4	-2

The combination for a sum of 7 is (-, 0, +)

  b. The sum of 0 + 8 gives you a Mannie's Number of -1

1 + 7	0
2 + 6	+2
3 + 5	-1

The combination for a sum of 8 is (-, 0, +)

16. **a.** 2 (TWO, FOUR, SIX) (FOUR, SIX, EIGHT)

72

b. 3 (FOUR, SIX, THREE) (FOUR, SEVEN, TWO) (FOUR, SEVEN, EIGHT)

c. 1 (THREE, FOUR, SEVEN)

17. FOUR, SIX, EIGHT, NINE

18. FIRST STEP: Taking G from EIGHT means the H must come from THREE.
ZERO, TWO, THREE, SIX, EIGHT

19. FIRST STEP: The letter H must come from a name in Column 3 on Chart 2.
THREE, FOUR, SIX

20. **a.** It is not possible. You will find the letter G in the name EIGHT, which will give you a Mannie's Number of +3. You will find the letter U in the name FOUR, with a Mannie's Number of 0, which in combination gives you a Mannie's Number of +3. The letter N is found in the name ONE (-2), SEVEN (+2), and NINE (+5). You will never find a name spelled with an N that in combination with EIGHT and FOUR will give you a - Mannie's Number.

b. It is possible. You will find the letters Z and O in the name ZERO, which has a Mannie's Number of -4. You will find the other letter O in the names ONE (-2), TWO (-1), and FOUR (0). All of these names, when each are in combination with the name ZERO, will give you a - Mannie's Number.

21. **a.** RUSH   THREE, FOUR, SIX

    b. ZENITH   ZERO, EIGHT, NINE

    c. GET   FOUR, SIX, EIGHT

    d. REFUGE   FOUR, FIVE, EIGHT

    e. TERROR   ZERO, THREE, FOUR

    f. WINTER   TWO, THREE, NINE

    g. SORT   ONE, THREE, SIX

22. **a.** FIRST STEP: I would take the letter U from the name FOUR, which has a Mannie's Number of 0.
TWO, THREE, FOUR, EIGHT

    b. FIRST STEP: Same as above.
ZERO,ONE, THREE, FOUR

23. **a.** FIRST STEP: Eleven letters and a +5 Mannie's Number gives a sum in ones of 16.
TWO, FIVE, NINE

    b. FIRST STEP: Five ones and a -6 Mannie's Number gives a total of eleven letters.
ZERO, ONE, FOUR

c. FIRST STEP: I would decide which columns on Chart 2 would give me the three digit names.
ZERO, THREE, FOUR

d. FIRST STEP: twenty ones and a +7 Mannie's Number gives a total of thirteen letters.
FOUR, SEVEN, NINE

24. FIRST STEP: I would find the U in the name FOUR, which means the letter F would come from the name FIVE, giving a combined Mannie's Number of +1.
ZERO, FOUR, FIVE, SEVEN

25. FIRST STEP: I would find the U in the name FOUR, which means the letter F would come from the name FIVE, using a total of eight letters.
TWO, THREE, FOUR, FIVE

26. FIRST STEP: I would find the letter W in the name TWO.
TWO, SEVEN, EIGHT

27. FIRST STEP: Decide which Chart to use. What is your choice?
The minimum number of letters for two names is six.
The maximum number of letters for two names is ten.

28. The answer will always be a + Mannie's Number, because there are more ones than letters.

29.   **a.** OXEN   SIX, ONE

          b. NOISE   SIX, ONE

c. THRONE   THREE, ONE

d. GONE   EIGHT, ONE

e. STONE   TWO, SEVEN

30. The third digit must be ZERO, which has a Mannie's Number of -4. The Mannie's Number for the combination of all three digit names is 0. The first two digits must have a Mannie's Number of +4. We know that these two digits have a total of thirteen ones, which means that there are nine letters in their combined names. The first two digits are FIVE and EIGHT (+4 and nine letters).
ZERO, FIVE, EIGHT

31. The third digit must be FOUR, which maintains the Mannie's Number of 0 for all three digits. We know that the sum in ones is 11, which also means that there are eleven letters in the three names. The name FOUR has four letters, so the first two digits must have seven letters and a total of seven ones. The first two digits are TWO and FIVE.
TWO, FOUR, FIVE

32.   **a.** SIGHT   SIX, EIGHT

       b. NIGHT   NINE, EIGHT

       c. TIGHT   THREE, EIGHT

       d. RIGHT   THREE, EIGHT

33. FIRST STEP: I made the observation that one of the digit names spelled with the letter T will have a unique letter.
TWO, THREE, FIVE, SEVEN

34. SUIT: U - FOUR, S - SIX or SEVEN, T - TWO, THREE, or EIGHT.
Yes, the letter T can come from the digit name TWO.
SUITE: U - FOUR, SI or SE - SIX or SEVEN, TE or IT - THREE or EIGHT
NO, the letter T cannot come from the digit name TWO.

35.
   a. The answer is two names. One letter O must come from a name with a unique letter.

   b. The answer is one name. Two names without the letter E will have a unique letter.

   c. The answer is two names. One of the names without the letter E will have a unique letter.

   d. FIRST STEP: All three digit names are spelled with the letter E. The answer is two names. The OE must come from the names ZERO and ONE.

36. Olivia is correct. One of the two names that is spelled with the letter I will also be spelled with the letter E.

37. The answer is NO. We are sure that you gave a great explanation for your choice.

BONUS ANSWERS

1. C will not have a unique letter. A, having a unique letter in its digit name, means that A is an even digit. B, not having a unique letter in its digit name, means that B is an odd digit. When you add an even and an odd digit, the sum is always odd.

2. X is ONE   Y is THREE   Z is FOUR   W is SEVEN

Z has no E in its spelling, which makes it an even digit; the choices being TWO, FOUR, and SIX. W is an odd digit, which makes Y and X also odd. TWO and SIX cannot be used for Z, as this would violate the equation rules.

Congratulations on completing the book. We knew you could do it! We hope that you have had as much fun answering the challenges and puzzles as we had developing them and investigating them with you. Don't forget to challenge yourself daily, using your new and improved thinking skills!

CHART 1

ZERO	ONE	TWO	THREE	FOUR	FIVE	SIX	SEVEN	EIGHT	NINE
0	1	2	3	4	5	6	7	8	9
	I	II	III	IIII	II III	III III	III IIII	IIII IIII	IIII IIIII

CHART 2

COLUMN 1	COLUMN 2	COLUMN 3
Names with three letters	Names with four letters	Names with five letters
ONE TWO SIX	ZERO FOUR FIVE NINE	THREE SEVEN EIGHT

	COLUMN 1	COLUMN 2	COLUMN 3	
Number of letters used	9	16	15	Total = 40 letters

CHART 3

	ZERO	ONE	TWO	THREE	FOUR	FIVE	SIX	SEVEN	EIGHT	NINE
	0	1	2	3	4	5	6	7	8	9
		I	II	III	IIII	II III	III III	III IIII	IIII IIII	IIII IIIII
Mannie's Number	-4	-2	-1	-2	0	+1	+3	+2	+3	+5

CHART 4

COLUMN 1	COLUMN 2	COLUMN 3	COLUMN 4
Letters	Amount found	Number of names in which it is found	Names
E	9	7	Zero, One, Three, Five, Seven, Eight, Nine
F	2	2	Four, Five
G	1	1	Eight
H	2	2	Three, Eight
I	4	4	Five, Six, Eight, Nine
N	4	3	One, Seven, Nine
O	4	4	Zero, One, Two, Four
R	3	3	Zero, Three, Four
S	2	2	Six, Seven
T	3	3	Two, Three, Eight
U	1	1	Four
V	2	2	Five, Seven
W	1	1	Two
X	1	1	Six
Z	1	1	Zero

FREQUENCY GRAPH

DISTRIBUTION OF THE 40 LETTERS USED TO SPELL THE DIGIT NAMES

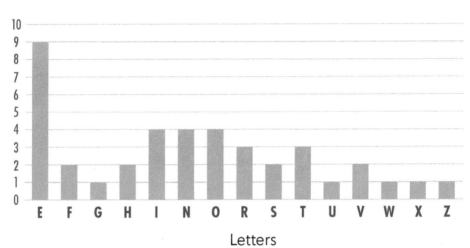

Number of Times Letter Appears

Letters

CHART 6

COLUMN 1	COLUMN 2
Names With Unique Letters	Names Without Unique Letters
ZERO	ONE
TWO	THREE
FOUR	FIVE
SIX	SEVEN
EIGHT	NINE

CHART 5

LETTERS	COLUMN 1 CHART 2 Column 1	COLUMN 2 CHART 2 Column 2	COLUMN 3 CHART 2 Column 3
E	✓	✓	✓
F		✓	
G			✓
H			✓
I	✓	✓	✓
N	✓	✓	✓
O	✓	✓	
R		✓	✓
S	✓		✓
T	✓		✓
U		✓	
V		✓	✓
W	✓		
X	✓		
Z		✓	

CPSIA information can be obtained
at www.ICGtesting.com
Printed in the USA
BVHW011515190323
660570BV00002B/4

9 781039 110298